CONTINENTS OF THE WORLD

AFRICA

Rob Bowden

First published in 2005 by Hodder Wayland,
an imprint of Hodder Children's Books

This paperback edition published in 2007 by Wayland,
an imprint of Hachette Children's Books

© Wayland 2005

Commissioning editor: Victoria Brooker
Editor: Kelly Davis
Inside design: Jane Hawkins
Cover design: Wayland

Series concept and project management
by EASI-Educational Resourcing
(info@easi-er.co.uk)
Statistical research: Anna Bowden

Population Distribution Map
© 2003 UT-Battelle, LLC. All rights reserved.
Data for population distribution maps reproduced under licence from UT-Battelle,
LLC.
All rights reserved.

Maps and graphs: Martin Darlison, Encompass Graphics

British Library Cataloguing in Publication Data

Rob Bowden
  Africa – (Continents of the world)
  1. Africa – Juvenile literature
  2.i. Title
  3.980

ISBN-13: 978 0 7502 5091 7

Printed and bound in China

Hachette Children's Books
338 Euston Road, London NW1 3BH

Picture acknowledgements
The author and publisher would like to thank the following for allowing their
pictures to be reproduced in this publication:
Corbis 6 and 11 (Bettmann), 7 (Gallo Images), 12 (Louise Gubb), 13, 37 and 51
(Reuters), 24 (Howard Davies), 35 (Inge Yspeert), 38 (Michael S. Lewis), 41 and
55 (Yann Arthus-Bertrand), 45 (Colin Garratt; Milepost 92 1/2), 52 (Patrick
Roberts), 53 (Dan Eldon), 57 (Staffan Widstrand), 58 (Adrian Arbib), 59(b)
Charles O'Rear; EASI-Images cover main, 3, title page, 8, 9(t), 14, 15, 16(b), 18,
20, 21, 23, 27, 29, 30, 31, 32, 36, 40, 46, 47, 48, 49(t), 49(b), 50, 54 and 59(t)
(Roy Maconachie), 4, 10, 16(t), 19, 22, 25, 26, 33, 42, 43, cover inset and 56
(Rob Bowden), 9(b) and 34 (Lorena Ros); Panos Pictures 39 (Jacob Silberberg);
Still Pictures 44 (Mark Edwards).

Main cover picture: A woman from the Pokot ethnic group of north western
Kenya. The Pokot are one of the few ethnic groups in Kenya to maintain
very strong cultural traditions due to their remote homelands in the Great Rift
Valley.

The website addresses (URLs) included in this book were valid at the time of
going to press. However, because of the nature of the Internet, it is possible that
some addresses may have changed, or sites may have changed or closed down
since publication. While the author and Publishers regret any inconvenience this
may cause the readers, no responsibility for any such changes can be accepted
by either the author or the Publisher.

Mount Toubkal (4,165 m/13,665 feet), in the High

Atlas mountains of Morocco.

CONTENTS

AFRICA – A MIGHTY CONTINENT

Africa is a vast continent covering 30,131,536 sq km (11,633,846 sq miles), or just over one-fifth of the Earth's land surface. It is so big that the United States and China could fit into it and still leave room for the whole of Europe! It is a continent of incredible people, amazing wildlife and breathtaking scenery. But Africa is also the world's poorest region – a continent that struggles with the problems of disease, hunger and war. A child born in Africa today will live on average for just 56 years – a full 21 years less than a child born in the United States or the UK, and seven years short of the global average.

EXTREME AFRICA

There are many extremes to be found within Africa. It has the world's largest desert (the Sahara), its longest river (the Nile) and one of its biggest geographical features (the Great Rift Valley). On the plains of East Africa, it has the greatest concentration of mammals anywhere on Earth. These include the giraffe, elephant and cheetah – the world's tallest, largest and fastest mammals. Africa's Congo rainforest (2,268,000 sq km/875,675 sq miles) is second only to the Amazon forest in South America, and Lake Victoria (69,484 sq km /26,828 sq miles) is only beaten in size by Lake Superior in North America.

Africa's people also experience economic extremes. In many of Africa's greatest cities, such as Cairo (Egypt), Lagos (Nigeria), Nairobi (Kenya) and Johannesburg (South Africa), incredible wealth is found side by side with some of the worst living conditions in the world. And there are cultural extremes in today's Africa, which blends ancient traditions with modern technology: many people follow customs dating back thousands of years, while working in air-conditioned offices and talking on mobile phones.

These contrasts have fascinated visitors to Africa for hundreds of years. To early traders and explorers, Africa was a 'Dark Continent' full of mystery, and even today it continues to surprise the outside world. This book will explore this mighty continent and reveal some of its secrets by introducing you to its landscapes, its people, its societies and its wildlife.

Despite centuries of change, markets remain a centre of activity in Africa. This one is in Kampala, Uganda.

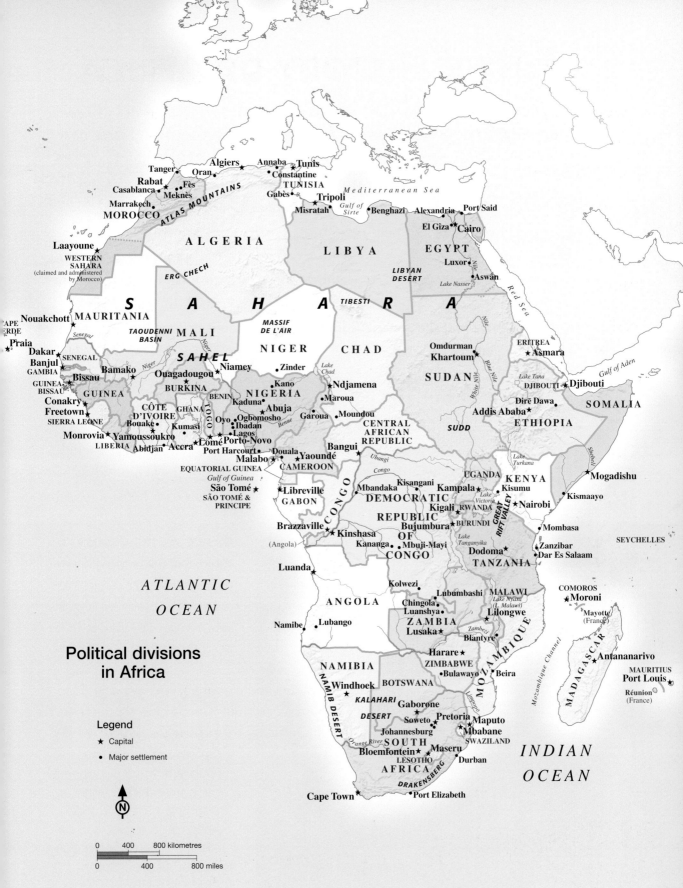

Tanger
Algiers
Annaba
Tunis
Oran
Constantine
Rabat
Fès
TUNISIA
Casablanca
Meknès
Gabès
Tripoli
Misratah
Gulf of
Sirte
Benghazi
Alexandria
Port Said
Marrakech
MOROCCO
ATLAS MOUNTAINS
Mediterranean Sea
El Gîza
Cairo

Laayoune
WESTERN
SAHARA
(claimed and administered
by Morocco)
ALGERIA
LIBYA
EGYPT
ERG CHECH
Luxor
LIBYAN
DESERT
Aswân
Lake Nasser
Red Sea

Nouakchott
MAURITANIA
S A H A R A
TIBESTI
TAOUDENNI
BASIN
MALI
Senegal
SAHEL
Niger
NIGER
MASSIF
DE L'AIR
CHAD
Omdurman
Khartoum
ERITREA
Asmara
CAPE
VERDE
Praia
Dakar
SENEGAL
Banjul
GAMBIA
Bamako
Niger
Ouagadougou
Niamey
Zinder
Lake
Chad
SUDAN
Blue Nile
Lake Tana
DJIBOUTI
Djibouti
Gulf of Aden
Bissau
GUINEA-
BISSAU
BURKINA
Kano
Ndjamena
SOMALIA
GUINEA
CÔTE
D'IVOIRE
BENIN
NIGERIA
Kaduna
Maroua
Dirè Dawa
Conakry
GHANA
Oyo
Ogbomosho
Abuja
Garoua
Moundou
Addis Ababa
ETHIOPIA
Freetown
SIERRA LEONE
Bouake
TOGO
Ibadan
Benue
White Nile
SUDD
Kumasi
Lagos
CENTRAL
AFRICAN
REPUBLIC
Monrovia
Yamoussoukro
Lomé
Porto-Novo
LIBERIA
Abidjan
Accra
Port Harcourt
Malabo
Douala
Yaoundé
Bangui
Lake
Turkana
Shebeli
Mogadishu
EQUATORIAL GUINEA
Gulf of Guinea
CAMEROON
Ubangi
UGANDA
KENYA
São Tomé
SÃO TOMÉ &
PRINCIPE
Libreville
GABON
Congo
Mbandaka
Kisangani
Kampala
Kisumu
Kismaayo
DEMOCRATIC
Lake
Victoria
Nairobi
Kigali
RWANDA
GREAT RIFT VALLEY
CONGO
REPUBLIC
OF
Bujumbura
BURUNDI
Mombasa
Brazzaville
Kinshasa
CONGO
Kananga
Mbuji-Mayi
Lake
Tanganyika
Dodoma
Zanzibar
Dar Es Salaam
SEYCHELLES
Luanda
TANZANIA
ATLANTIC
Kolwezi
COMOROS
Moroni
OCEAN
ANGOLA
Lubumbashi
MALAWI
Lake Nyasa
(L. Malawi)
Mayotte
(France)
Chingola
Luanshya
Lilongwe
Namibe
Lubango
ZAMBIA
Zambezi
Blantyre
Antananarivo
Lusaka
MADAGASCAR
MAURITIUS
Port Louis
Harare
Political divisions
in Africa
NAMIBIA
ZIMBABWE
Bulawayo
Beira
Réunion
(France)
NAMIB DESERT
BOTSWANA
Windhoek
KALAHARI
DESERT
Gaborone
Soweto
Pretoria
Maputo
Mbabane
SWAZILAND
Legend
★ Capital
• Major settlement
Orange River
Johannesburg
SOUTH
AFRICA
Bloemfontein
Maseru
LESOTHO
Durban
INDIAN
OCEAN
N
DRAKENSBERG
0   400   800 kilometres
0   400   800 miles
Cape Town
Port Elizabeth

1. THE HISTORY OF AFRICA

AFRICA IS AN ANCIENT CONTINENT. IT WAS ONCE THE CENTRE OF 'Pangaea', a super-continent that existed over 250 million years ago, when all today's continents were joined, forming one enormous landmass. Around 180 million years ago, movements in vast interlocking sheets of rock in the Earth's crust known as plates, began to break Pangaea apart. Africa remained fairly stationary, but other landmasses drifted thousands of kilometres to form the continents we know today. This is why, on a map of the world, the coastlines of Africa and the Americas look as if they could fit together like pieces of a giant jigsaw puzzle.

ORIGINS OF LIFE

Africa is the place where life on Earth began. The earliest living organisms, the oldest dinosaur eggs, the earliest known mammals and the oldest fish all come from Africa. Archaeologists have also unearthed what they believe to be the earliest evidence of our own human ancestors

Mary and Louis Leakey examine fragments of skull belonging to early human ancestors. The Leakeys made discoveries in Tanzania and Kenya that show Africa to be the birthplace of the first human beings.

FACT FILE

The Coelacanth is the oldest known fish. (Coelacanth fossils dating back over 360 million years have been found.) Although presumed to be extinct, a Coelacanth was caught alive off South Africa in 1938.

in Africa. The oldest remains date back 4.5 million years to a time when our ancestors (known collectively as 'hominoids') were perhaps closer to today's gorillas and chimpanzees than they were to modern humans.

Some of the most important hominoid discoveries were made in eastern Africa, in Ethiopia, Kenya and Tanzania. These show that by around 2.5 million years ago our ancestors had learned to walk upright and to make basic stone tools. The first man-made shelters appeared around 1.75 million years ago, and by about 1.5 million years ago hominoids had learned how to cook. *Homo erectus* was the first hominoid to leave Africa and spread into Asia and Europe between 1.8 and 0.5 million years ago. Modern humans (*Homo sapiens sapiens*) did not emerge from Africa until around 100,000 years ago. They gradually spread across the world, reaching Australia about 50,000 years ago and the Americas as recently as 15,000 years ago. As *Homo sapiens sapiens*, we are the only surviving and most successful hominoid. Since those first steps taken by our ancient African ancestors, we have colonized almost every part of our planet.

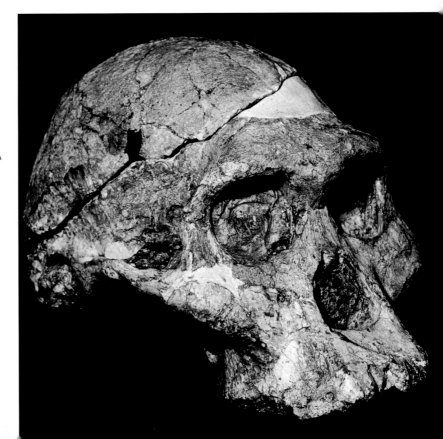

The skull of *Australopithecus africanus* – one of the earliest known hominoids found in Africa.

EARLY HUMANS IN AFRICA

At the mouth of the River Klasies in South Africa, there is evidence of early human activity dating back 120,000 years. This shows that humans at this time began to catch fish from the sea, in addition to hunting and gathering from the land. They had developed sophisticated tools made from wood and stone and learned to use fire for cooking and drying food. The world's earliest art also comes from Africa and dates back 100,000 years or more. Charcoal and ochre rock paintings have been found in Namibia and South Africa, while in Ethiopia shells were used to make what appears to be early jewellery.

Thousands of years later, the Sahara was an important centre of population in Africa, as shown by rock paintings dating from 8000 to 6000 BC. The Sahara region was much wetter then than it is today and animals such as hippopotamus, giraffe and elephant were common. These paintings also show that humans took some of the first steps towards farming cattle and growing crops during this period.

Rock art, such as this example in the Sahara desert of Algeria, provides historians with clues about early human settlement in Africa.

FACT FILE

The building of the Great Pyramid of Pharoah Khufu in Egypt required a highly organized workforce. Thousands of people spent over twenty years cutting, moving and arranging some 2.3 million stone blocks, each weighing around 2.5 tonnes (2.5 tons)!

AFRICAN CIVILIZATIONS

The next phase in Africa's history was dominated by the great civilization of ancient Egypt. This began in around 3100 BC and reached its height between 2700 and 1200 BC. The ancient Egyptians lived around the River Nile in the area that is modern-day Egypt, but they had trade links that extended deep into the rest of Africa and neighbouring Asia. The pharaohs (the rulers of ancient Egypt) accumulated great wealth and built grand settlements, palaces and tombs. Several of these structures can still be seen today. The most famous are the pyramids of Giza. The Great Pyramid built for the Pharaoh Khufu is the largest of these and was built in around 2550 BC.

Africa's other civilizations did not emerge until well after the end of the Egyptian civilization, and none was ever on the same scale. Among the most significant were the early West African states of Ghana (AD 600), Mali (AD 1200), Hausa (AD 1200)

The Great Pyramid of Pharaoh Khufu is one of ancient Egypt's greatest monuments, dating back over 4,500 years.

A replica of one of the Benin bronzes – beautiful heads that were fashioned during the Benin empire in what is now Nigeria.

Fort Jesus in Mombassa, Kenya, was built by the Portuguese in 1593 and later occupied by Arab and British conquerors. It is a lasting mark of foreign interests in Africa.

FACT FILE

The Spanish territories of Ceuta and Melilla, on the North African coast, are the only parts of Africa that remain under European control. They were originally established by the Portuguese, in 1415 and 1497 respectively.

and Benin (AD 1250). These civilizations all benefited from the trans-Saharan trade routes that transported gold, salt, ivory and slaves between West Africa and North Africa and the Middle East.

EUROPEAN EXPANSION

In 1415, the Portuguese established a trading post at Ceuta on the North African coast. This began the process of European expansion into Africa that was to last until the mid-twentieth century. By the mid-1500s, the Portuguese had coastal trading posts stretching from modern-day Morocco in the north-west to Kenya in the east. Africa provided Portugal with great riches, in the form of gold, ivory, hides, spices and slaves.

By 1600 other European nations were starting to compete for a share of Africa's riches, and by the 1800s British, Dutch, French and other European powers had all established coastal trading posts. The slave trade was particularly important because it provided labour for European and later US-owned sugar and cotton plantations in the Americas and the Caribbean. It has been estimated that up to 27 million Africans were sold or died as slaves between the late sixteenth and mid-nineteenth centuries.

THE SCRAMBLE FOR AFRICA

By 1870, European powers in Africa had yet to penetrate far beyond their coastal trading posts. The interior of the continent was defended by local tribal groups, and tropical diseases killed or weakened those Europeans who dared to venture inland. This changed by the end of the nineteenth century, when scientific and technological breakthroughs, such as the development of superior weapons and medical advances, at last enabled the European powers to conquer the heart of Africa. In 1885 Britain, France, Portugal and other European nations met in Berlin and carved Africa up between themselves. Over the next 70 to 80 years, European powers colonized almost every part of the continent in a process that became known as 'the scramble for Africa'.

By 1914, the entire continent, apart from Ethiopia, South Africa and Liberia, was under European colonial control. New cities grew up and railways and roads were built to link them to the coastal ports. These transport networks were used to export Africa's agricultural and mineral wealth (including cotton, tea, rubber, cocoa, diamonds,

Men, women and children captured by slave hunters in Zanzibar are tied together and marched to market, where they will be sold to slave traders.

copper and gold) back to the colonial powers in Europe, where it could be processed into food or manufactured goods. This 'extractive' pattern continued throughout the colonial period in Africa and still does today.

INDEPENDENT AFRICA

Following the cost and destruction of the Second World War (1939-45), European nations began to view their colonies in Africa as a burden. Meanwhile, Africans began to organize themselves and campaign for independence from Europe. In 1957, Gold Coast became the first black African nation to gain independence (from Britain) when it was renamed Ghana. A further 35 colonies gained their independence by 1970. In the mid-1970s, another eight colonies become independent, sometimes after a violent struggle. The Mozambique Liberation Front (FRELIMO), for example, began an armed conflict in 1964 with its Portuguese colonizers, before Frelimo finally won independence for Mozambique in 1975. Zimbabwe (1980), Namibia (1990) and Eritrea (1993) later also gained independence, completing the modern political map of Africa.

POLITICS AND CONFLICT

High hopes for independent Africa were disappointed, as the new states quickly became caught up in internal conflicts. Between 1960 and 2003, African countries experienced 107 coups, wars or invasions that led to a change of leadership. Millions of Africans have died in the process and corrupt leaders have robbed their nations of millions of dollars. For example, Mobutu Sese Seko, who ruled the

Nelson Mandela greets supporters in 1993. Mandela's release from prison in 1990, and the end of apartheid which followed it, were two of the most important events in Africa's recent history.

Democratic Republic of the Congo (then Zaire) between 1965 and 1997, is said to have amassed a personal fortune of over US$4 billion, while his people suffered appalling poverty. Corruption and conflict have made Africa an unstable, impoverished region, with many nations worse off today than they were when they gained independence.

●●●●●● ▶ IN FOCUS: Apartheid

Apartheid (meaning 'keep apart') was a policy introduced by the White minority government of South Africa in 1948. It created a society in which Coloureds and Blacks were denied the right to vote and were barred from the schools, hospitals, residential areas and even parks used by White South Africans. Some South Africans formed groups to resist apartheid, but they were often brutally suppressed by the government. Many of their leaders, including Nelson Mandela, were imprisoned. Mandela became an international symbol of the struggle against apartheid. Many nations refused to trade with South Africa until, in 1990, the government finally began to abolish apartheid and released Mandela and other prisoners. In 1994, South Africa held its first free elections and Nelson Mandela became President. Although the White minority government has gone, the divisions caused by over forty years of apartheid still remain a barrier to a truly unified South Africa.

Strand beach, near Cape Town, South Africa, 1988: A Black worker pushes a cart laden with rubbish past a beach reserved for Whites under South Africa's apartheid laws.

2. AFRICAN ENVIRONMENTS

*F*ROM SNOW-CAPPED MOUNTAINS AND TROPICAL FORESTS TO VAST grasslands and hostile deserts, Africa has an incredible diversity of environments. It also has some of the most spectacular landscape features in the world, including the Great Rift Valley in eastern Africa, Table Mountain in South Africa and Victoria Falls on the border of Zimbabwe and Zambia.

The Sahara desert, here in Niger, is the largest desert in the world and rarely has any rainfall. It is a hyper-arid environment.

WHERE THERE IS NO RAIN

Africa is often thought of as a very dry land. To the outside world, drought and famine appear to be almost permanent features of life here. However, while much of Africa is generally arid (dry), this is by no means true of the whole continent. The Congo rainforest and Cameroon highlands, for example, experience well over 2,000 mm (80 inches) of rainfall each year. It is mainly this variation in the availability of water that has led to the development of different African environments.

DRYLANDS

Around two-thirds of Africa is classified as a dryland environment. Drylands are areas of low and unreliable rainfall and are broken down into different types according to how arid (dry) they are. Hyper-arid environments receive virtually no rainfall at all and are more commonly known as deserts. In Africa, deserts cover about 22 per cent of the continent and include the Sahara in North Africa and the Kalahari and Namib deserts in south-west Africa. Very few people live in such hyper-arid environments and those who

do are gathered around a few water sources such as oases or river valleys. The Nile Valley in Egypt is a good example of this. With so much of Egypt classified as desert, most of the people are crowded into a narrow strip of land that stretches just a few kilometres on either side of the Nile. River water is used to irrigate this land, to make up for the lack of natural rainfall.

Arid and semi-arid environments cover around 55 per cent of Africa. Annual rainfall in these regions is typically less than 100 mm (4 inches) for arid areas and 100-600 mm (4-24 inches) per year in semi-arid environments. Even more problematic than low rainfall, however, is unreliable rainfall. An arid area may receive 500 mm (20 inches) in one year, but then no rain at all for over ten years. This makes life very difficult for the estimated one-third of Africa's population living in arid and semi-arid environments. At its most extreme, an extended period of dryness can lead to drought and famine and displace millions from their homes.

AFRICA'S MOUNTAINS

Many of Africa's highest peaks were once active volcanoes. At 5,895 m (19,340 feet), Mount Kilimanjaro in Tanzania is high enough to have glaciers and snow on its summit, despite standing

People exist in semi-arid areas by adapting to the environment. This pastoralist in Burkina Faso has brought his cattle to drink at a seasonal water source.

Mount Kilimanjaro provides a dramatic backdrop to the savannah plains of Tanzania and Kenya.

almost on the equator. The main mountainous regions of Africa are the Ruwenzori range in western Uganda, the Atlas mountains in Morocco and Tunisia, the Ethiopian highlands and the Drakensberg range in South Africa. Although not as populated as other areas, the Atlas mountains and the Ethiopian highlands both support significant populations. The people living in the Atlas mountains are known as Berbers and are highly skilled at living in mountain environments. They have a system of terracing the slopes that allows them to capture rainfall and cultivate a wide range of crops including wheat, barley, fruits, vegetables, nuts and olives. Others are nomadic pastoralists and travel across the mountains with herds of sheep, goats and cattle to pastures that have been used for hundreds of years.

LAKES AND RIVERS

Lake Victoria is Africa's largest lake, covering an area of 69,484 sq km (26,828 sq miles). Other major lakes include Lake Tanganyika (Tanzania), Lake Malawi (Malawi), Lake Turkana (Kenya) and Lake Chad (Chad). There are also several artificial lakes formed by the construction of dams. Lake Nasser in Egypt and Sudan, Lake Volta in Ghana and Lake Kariba in Zimbabwe are among the largest.

FACT FILE

Victoria Falls, on the Zambezi river in southern Africa, is among the world's biggest waterfalls. It is 1,700 m (5,577 feet) wide and 108 m (354 feet) tall at its highest point. The roar of its water can be heard up to 40 km (25 miles) away.

The force of the Zambezi river has cut enormous gorges into the landscape as it crashes over Victoria Falls.

The Nile is Africa's greatest river and the longest in the world.
It stretches for 6,650 km (4,132 miles) across the continent, from
Burundi in Central Africa to Egypt in the north, and drains water
from all or part of nine African countries. At 4,700 km (2,920
miles), the Congo is Africa's second-longest river and actually
drains an area (known as a drainage basin) slightly larger than

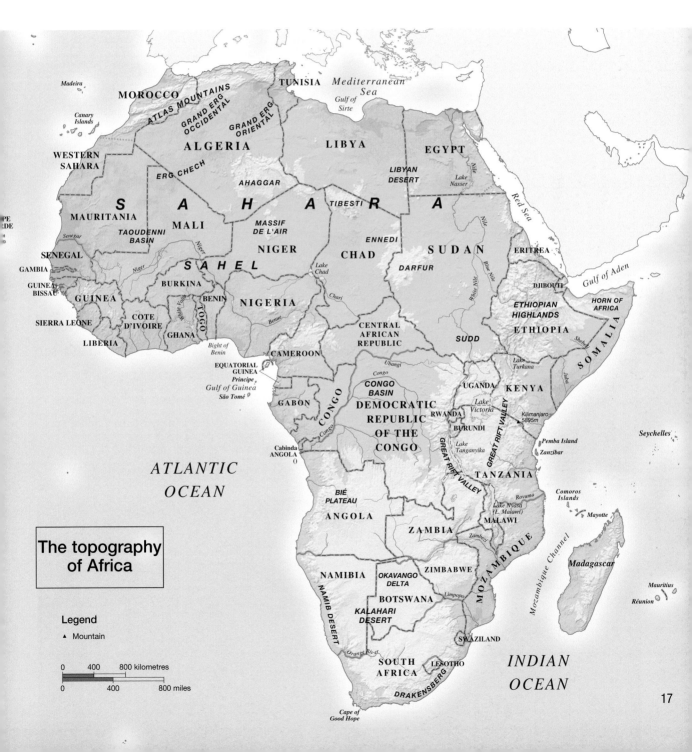

The topography of Africa

Legend

▲ Mountain

0   400   800 kilometres

0   400   800 miles

the Nile. Between them, these two rivers drain around a fifth of the continent. Africa's other major rivers are the Niger in West Africa and the Zambezi and Orange rivers in southern Africa.

PLATEAU LANDS

Much of Africa consists of mainly flat areas known as plateaus. In southern and eastern Africa, many plateaus are at high altitude. For example, Nairobi (the capital of Kenya) lies on a plateau at an altitude of 1,661 m (5,450 feet). The plateaus of northern and western Africa are at a lower altitude and in the extreme north they extend into lowland coastal plains. The coastal region of Egypt is so low that, if sea levels were to rise as a result of global warming, much of it would be flooded by the Mediterranean Sea.

FORESTS AND GRASSLANDS

Forests cover an area of around 3,766,000 sq km (1,454,000 sq miles) in Africa, or around 12.5 per cent of the total land area. The largest single area of forest is the Congo rainforest, which occupies about 2,268,000 sq km (875,675 sq miles) in Central Africa. There are also patches of tropical rainforest in a broad band across the continent, from Kenya in the east to the Gambia in the west. Others include the evergreen forests of highland regions, and the dryland forests which are dominated by species such as acacia trees. Another type of forest common in Africa is known as a savannah woodland (or 'Miombo' in southern Africa). This is a thinly spaced forest that allows enough light in

An aerial walkway allows visitors to get up close to a tropical rainforest in Nigeria, West Africa. Tropical forests are some of the most species-rich environments on Earth.

for grassland to grow on the forest floor. Such forests are often found alongside larger areas of grassland or savannah. These include world-famous wildlife reserves such as the Masai Mara in Kenya and the Serengeti in Tanzania.

SPECIAL ENVIRONMENTS

Africa has several special environments, some of which are home to wildlife found nowhere else on Earth, such as the gelada (like a baboon) of the Ethiopian highlands and the lemurs of Madagascar's forests. Other special environments include the vast wetlands of the Sudd – a giant watery landscape that forms part of the Nile in southern Sudan. The Okavango Delta is another wetland in Botswana and is famous as the world's only inland delta. In East Africa there are the soda lakes of the Great Rift Valley, such as Lakes Nakuru, Natron, Magadi and Bogoria. These are more saline (salty) than normal lakes because they have no outlet, and high rates of evaporation in the hot climate concentrate the mineral salts, such as sodium carbonate, in the water. Also in East Africa is the Ngorongoro Crater, which is an extinct volcanic caldera. The crater covers 254 sq km (98 sq miles) and has walls that reach over 600 m (1,968 feet) in height.

Herbivores, such as these topi and gazelle, thrive on the savannah grasslands of the Masai Mara in Kenya. They provide food, in turn, for Africa's predators, including the lion, leopard and cheetah.

FACT FILE

Africa's Great Rift Valley is around 6,400 km (3,977 miles) long and has an average width of 50-65 km (30-40 miles). The valley walls climb an average of 600-900 m (1,968-2,952 feet) to the surrounding highlands.

Dark clouds on the horizon signal the approach of the rains off the Atlantic coastline of Sierra Leone in West Africa.

Some of the world's most species-rich coral reefs are located off the coasts of East Africa and Egypt. Africa also has important areas of mangrove swamp – a form of semi-submerged forest that grows in coastal waters. Like coral reefs, mangroves are very rich in wildlife and provide breeding grounds for many bird and fish species.

THE SHIFTING RAINS

Africa's rains are greatly affected by the inter-tropical convergence zone (ITCZ). At this point in the tropics, the north-east and south-west trade winds meet, and warm air and moisture are forced upwards, creating a band of heavy rain clouds and thunderstorms. As the months pass, the ITCZ moves towards the hottest landmass, following the seasonal movement of the sun. It moves north between March and August, when the sun is in the northern hemisphere, and south between September and February, as the sun moves into the southern hemisphere. Much of Africa therefore has two rainy seasons per year as the ITCZ moves north and then south. The exception to this is in the far north and south of the continent, where the ITCZ reaches its limits before reversing direction. Africa's farmers try to time their farming around the movement of the ITCZ, but its arrival is extremely unpredictable. If the rains come early they can damage crops that are yet to be harvested, and if they are late newly planted seeds may already have withered and died.

Temperatures in Africa are generally warm and stable, although the south and north of the continent experience a wider variation in temperature at different times of year. Altitude also influences temperatures in Africa, with the average temperature falling by around 0.6°C (1.1°F) for every 100 m (328 foot) increase in altitude. This is known as the lapse rate and explains why Nairobi, Kenya, at around 1,600 m (5,250 feet), is several degrees cooler than Mombassa on the coast.

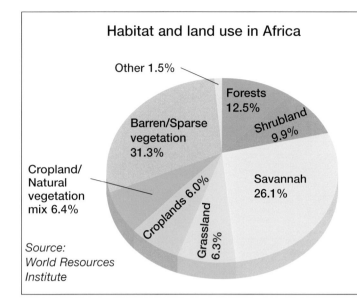

Habitat and land use in Africa

Other 1.5%
Forests 12.5%
Shrubland 9.9%
Barren/Sparse vegetation 31.3%
Savannah 26.1%
Cropland/ Natural vegetation mix 6.4%
Croplands 6.0%
Grassland 6.3%

Source: World Resources Institute

IN FOCUS: Desertification

The process of desertification – in which environments become more like deserts – is one of the most important environmental trends in Africa. Human actions, such as overgrazing and the removal of vegetation, are partly to blame. These encourage erosion and can turn fertile land into barren dust. Experts also blame climate change and believe that Africa's deserts are expanding as the continent becomes hotter and drier. Desertification is estimated to affect 46 per cent of Africa's land area, populated by over 500 million people. In Botswana almost a quarter of the land is at severe risk, and in semi-arid West Africa the desert is moving southwards by up to 5 km (3 miles) per year. In an already dry continent, desertification presents a major challenge for Africa in the twenty-first century.

Desertification, seen here in the Algerian town of Insula, threatens farmland and settlements across Africa.

3. THE PEOPLE OF AFRICA

AFRICA HAS THE FASTEST-GROWING POPULATION OF ANY CONTINENT. In fact, after Asia, it is the most populous continent in the world. Its population of 850.6 million in 2003 was nearly four times greater than in 1950. In a continent that many experts believe is already overpopulated, Africa's population is expected to more than double within the next 50 years – to over 1.8 billion by 2050. The population of Africa is not evenly distributed, however, and just three countries (Nigeria, Egypt and Ethiopia) account for nearly a third of its people.

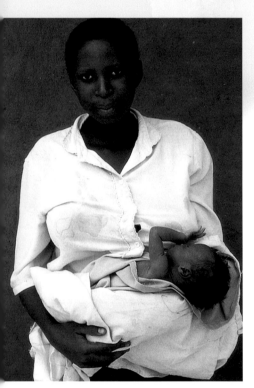

A Ugandan teenager cradles her new-born baby. Uganda has the youngest population in the world.

FACT FILE

In 2003, just over 1 in 8 of the world's people were African. By 2050, this is expected to increase to more than a fifth of the global population.

YOUTHFUL POPULATION

One of the reasons for Africa's rapid population growth is that it has the world's youngest population. This means that, even if population growth rates slow down, the total population will continue to increase for many years as today's children grow up and start families of their own. In 2002, around 49 per cent of Africa's population was under 18 years of age, compared to a global average of 35 per cent and 22 per cent in more developed nations such as the United States, Japan, Germany and the UK. One explanation for this youthful population is Africa's very low life expectancy, which averaged just 56 years in 2002 (and was below 34 in Zimbabwe and Zambia).

POOR HEALTH

Africa suffers from some of the poorest health conditions in the world. This is due to a combination of diseases (such as malaria) and a lack of health facilities and trained health professionals. Many of the most serious health problems are made worse by lack of clean water and sanitation. In sub-Saharan Africa, 43 per cent of the population had no access to safe water in 2000, and 47 per cent lacked basic sanitation. In such conditions, illnesses such as diarrhoea, cholera and typhoid can spread easily. Young children are especially at risk because their immune systems are weak. Each year in Africa an estimated 850,000 children die from diarrhoea – an entirely preventable illness. Many more children die from diseases that could be avoided through vaccinations or improvements in living conditions. In the continent as a whole, healthcare is so poor that in ten countries (including Mali, Sierra Leone and the Democratic Republic of the Congo) more than 1 in 5 children will die before reaching their fifth birthdays. In general, healthcare in North Africa is better than in sub-Saharan Africa. A Libyan or Tunisian born today, for example, can expect to outlive a Zambian or Zimbabwean by around 28 years.

KILLERS IN THE NIGHT

Malaria, transmitted by the bite of the female Anopheles mosquito, is one of Africa's biggest health problems. Mosquitoes are found almost everywhere in sub-Saharan Africa and are most active from

This channel in Kano, northern Nigeria, has become polluted because of the city's failure to keep pace with its growing population.

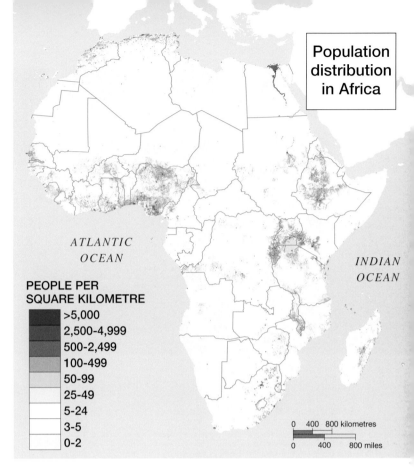

Population distribution in Africa

ATLANTIC
OCEAN

INDIAN
OCEAN

PEOPLE PER
SQUARE KILOMETRE

- >5,000
- 2,500-4,999
- 500-2,499
- 100-499
- 50-99
- 25-49
- 5-24
- 3-5
- 0-2

0   400   800 kilometres
0   400   800 miles

FACT FILE

Nigeria is Africa's most populous nation, with 124 million people in 2003. This means that more than 1 in every 7 Africans is a Nigerian.

An anti-malaria kit on sale in Tanzania.

dusk to dawn, so most people are bitten while they are sleeping. Malaria kills around a million people every year in Africa and affects millions more. It is also costly. Treating malaria patients has been estimated to cost African health systems US$12 billion a year.

Anti-malarial drugs are expensive and not always effective. But preventive measures, such as sleeping under a mosquito net to reduce the chances of being bitten, are highly effective, especially if the net is treated with insecticide. The cost of a treated net has fallen in recent years to about US$5, but this is still too expensive for most families. In 1999-2001, only 15 per cent of young children (those most at risk) were sleeping under a mosquito net, and just 2 per cent were using treated nets. In 1998, a global campaign called 'Roll Back Malaria' was launched, with the aim of halving the number of malaria deaths (90 per cent of which occur in Africa) by 2010. Governments and international agencies have pledged to spend more on disease prevention and treatment to try and meet these targets. In addition, scientists are searching for a vaccine to prevent malaria infection. But developing new vaccines is extremely expensive, and few Africans could afford to pay for them even if they became available.

EDUCATION FOR CHANGE

Like healthcare, education in Africa is of a low standard compared to elsewhere in the world. For example, in 2000 around 30 per cent of men and almost half of women in sub-Saharan Africa were illiterate (unable to read or write). This is unlikely to improve in the coming

• • • • • • ➤ IN FOCUS: HIV/AIDS

In 2003, over 29 million people in Africa were living with HIV/AIDS – 75 per cent of the global total. HIV/AIDS is most widespread among the working age population and so harms Africa's economy as well as its health. A particular problem is the number of children who are orphaned when their parents die of the disease. By 2002, over 11 million children under 15 years of age had been orphaned because of HIV/AIDS in Africa, and by 2010 this is expected to exceed 20 million. There is no cure for HIV/AIDS, but there are drugs that help to prolong the life of those infected. At present, these drugs are very expensive because they are controlled by a few large companies. Local companies could produce cheaper drugs, but even these might be beyond the reach of many Africans. Most health experts agree that the problem will get much worse in Africa over the coming decades unless a cure is found.

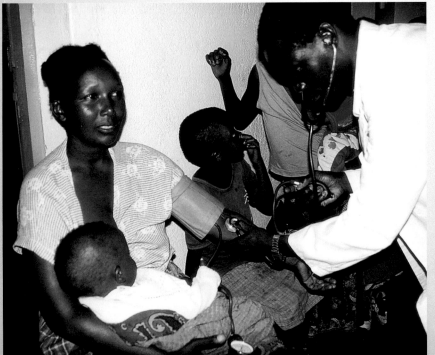

Rural clinics, such as this one in northern Kenya, offer only basic healthcare. They are ill-equipped to deal with Africa's HIV/AIDS epidemic.

years because school attendance levels in the region are low. In 2000, just 63 per cent of boys and 58 per cent of girls were enrolled in primary school and around a third of entrants left before completing their basic primary education (grade 5). Most children miss out on education because it costs too much. Even when governments pay the school fees, parents must find money for books, stationery, uniforms and meals. Another reason is that children may be required to help care for family members or to contribute to the family income by working in the fields or in factories and stores. Girls, in particular, are often kept away from school because of family commitments.

Improving education would dramatically benefit the people of Africa. Basic education (especially of girls) leads to improvements in health and a reduction in diseases. Education also reduces the rate of population growth, as people learn how to plan their families through the use of contraceptives. It is noticeable that in North African countries such as Tunisia,

Primary classes in Africa are often overcrowded and under-resourced. Many children fail to complete their primary schooling, with still fewer completing further studies.

FACT FILE

Only 0.02 per cent of Africa's land area is classified as built-up or urban.

Algeria and Libya, where education levels are higher (more often to secondary level), population growth is lower and health is considerably better. High costs mean that relatively few students go to university in Africa, but demand is increasing rapidly and new universities are opening across the continent. Cairo, in Egypt, has over 300,000 students at several universities. In Ghana, the number of universities increased from 4 to 12 between 1990 and 2001, and the student numbers grew from under 10,000 to around 44,000. However, despite such growth, Africa still has the lowest university attendances in the world, with, on average, fewer than 5 per cent of 19- to 24-year-olds enrolled.

A RURAL CONTINENT

Africa is the least urbanized continent in the world, with just 37 per cent of its population living in towns or cities at the start of the twenty-first century. This compares to a world average of 47 per cent, and over 73 per cent in Europe, Oceania and the

The Egyptian capital, Cairo, is Africa's largest city, with a population of at least 12 million people.

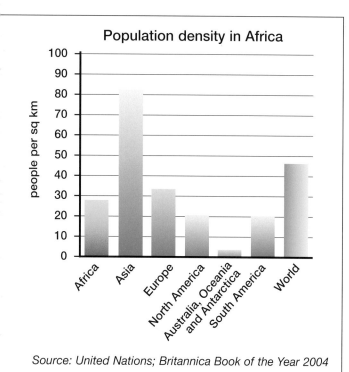

Population density in Africa

people per sq km

Source: United Nations; Britannica Book of the Year 2004

Americas. East Africa is the most rural part of the continent, with over 80 per cent of the population living in the countryside in Uganda, Ethiopia and Rwanda. Northern and southern Africa are less rural – 43 per cent of South Africans and 12 per cent of Libyans live in rural areas.

SERVICE PROVISION

Africa's rural population is scattered in small villages, many of which are not connected to transport networks. The lack of electricity and telephones in most rural areas adds to the problems. In such circumstances, it can take several days for essential supplies, such as medicines, to reach rural clinics. Because of difficulties like these, the standard of education and health tends to be much lower in rural areas. In Kenya, for example, 88 per cent of the urban population have access to safe water, compared to just 42 per cent of the rural population. Such inequalities encourage millions of Africans to migrate from rural to urban areas every year. They go in search of a better life, but in most cases they simply add to the problems of Africa's already struggling cities.

LIFE IN THE SLUMS

Lagos in Nigeria and Cairo in Egypt are among the largest cities in the world, each with a population of over ten million. Like many cities in Africa, however, they have been unable to cope with the rate of their growth. As a result, over half of their populations live in settlements known as shanty-towns or slums. Across Africa, such slums are home to an estimated 300 million urban Africans. Slum housing is usually built by the residents themselves, using whatever materials are available. It

is normally of poor quality and lacks services such as water, sanitation and electricity. In the Kibera slum of Nairobi, Kenya, for example, an estimated 750,000 people share just 600 toilets.

Slum housing, shown here in Freetown, Sierra Leone, is a familiar sight in many African cities. Migrants often have little choice but to settle in these areas.

CITIES FOR THE FUTURE

Cities are important to Africa and generate around 60 per cent of the continent's income, but their uncontrolled growth threatens many countries' stability. Several governments have recognized this fact and are working with slum communities and other organizations to improve urban life. Loan programmes have been started to help people set up businesses. And electricity, sanitation and water are now being provided for some slums. In Kenya, the government is giving people rights to land they have occupied if they promise to build proper homes, schools and community facilities. With over 50 per cent of Africans likely to live in urban areas by 2025, such improvements are essential to avoid future problems (such as disease or political instability) caused by poor living conditions.

FACT FILE

In 2003, an estimated 72 per cent of sub-Saharan Africa's urban residents lived in slums.

NATIONS OR TRIBES?

Africa is a continent of diverse ethnic groups or tribes. This diversity can be seen (or rather heard) in the estimated 2,035 languages spoken on the continent – almost a third of the world total. Ethiopia alone has over eighty spoken languages, while Nigeria has over five hundred. The colonial period saw Africa's ethnic groups thrown together or split apart by the newly established European boundaries that form the basis of Africa's modern nation states. This action has contributed to the turmoil that has existed in many African countries since independence. Forced to share the same territory, rival ethnic groups have struggled to gain power, often with violent consequences. In 1994, for instance, long-standing rivalry between the Hutu and Tutsi people in Rwanda erupted into violence that led to over 800,000 people being killed.

NORTH-SOUTH DIVIDE

The ethnic composition of Africa is more complex and varied than in any other continent. However, it is possible to make broad distinctions between the people of North and sub-Saharan Africa. In northern Africa, most people are of lighter skin colour, share physical characteristics with people of southern Europe and the Middle East, and speak mainly Arabic or one of the other Semitic languages (a family of Afro-Asiatic languages).

South of the Sahara, people's skin tone darkens considerably, because of more intense exposure to the sun. Most people in sub-Saharan Africa speak one of a family of languages known as Bantu. However, where northern and southern Africa meet, there is a complex mix of languages, and a third family

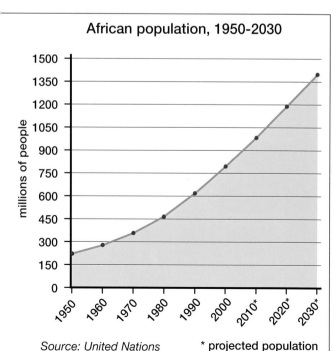

African population, 1950-2030

millions of people

Source: United Nations   * projected population

These traders in Sierra Leone share physical and language characteristics with people across much of sub-Saharan Africa.

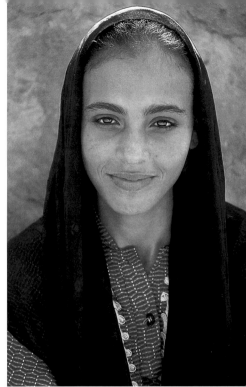

This young Egyptian woman speaks Arabic and has the lighter skin colouring that is characteristic of most North Africans.

of languages (known as Nilotic or Nilo-Saharan) is found. In southern Africa, Khoisan is another language family. This is spoken by the people of the Kalahari desert, such as the San (bushmen) and is famous for its use of 'clicks'. Madagascar also has its own languages (Malagasy), which are related to the Indonesian languages of Asia and probably developed through trade.

SETTLERS

Africa also has a settler population, most of whom were born in Africa as descendants of European colonists in the nineteenth and twentieth centuries. The most distinct settler group is the Afrikaner or Boer population of South Africa. They are descended from Dutch colonists who first arrived in the former Dutch colony of the Cape of Good Hope in 1652. They have developed their own language (Afrikaans) and culture, and make up around 10 per cent of South Africa's population. Other (mainly European) settler populations exist in Kenya, Zambia, Zimbabwe, Namibia and Mozambique.

FACT FILE

With so many local languages, most African countries have adopted an official national language, often linked to their colonial past. English is an official language in 20 countries and French in 21. Arabic is an official language for 16 countries and Portuguese for 3.

4. AFRICAN CULTURE AND RELIGION

PEOPLE OFTEN TALK ABOUT 'AFRICAN MUSIC', 'AFRICAN DANCE' and 'African food', but in reality Africa has many different cultures. The continent is a mosaic of different ethnic groups, each with their own particular traditions that have been passed down over hundreds of years.

ARTISTIC AFRICA

Art plays a central role in social, spiritual and political life in Africa. For example, it is often associated with ceremonies celebrating a child's entry into adulthood, or used to signify status through body art, clothing or accessories. Art is also historically important and, in the absence of written documents, it is sometimes the only link between Africa's past and its present. Sculpture, costume, dance and music are perhaps the most widespread art forms in Africa. But even everyday items, such as brightly painted taxis or beautifully decorated bowls and cooking utensils, become artistic expressions. The best-known works of art in Africa are masks and figures. These are normally carved from wood and then decorated with natural dyes or inlaid bone, ivory or metals. Some parts of Africa are well known for using other materials. The Nok culture of

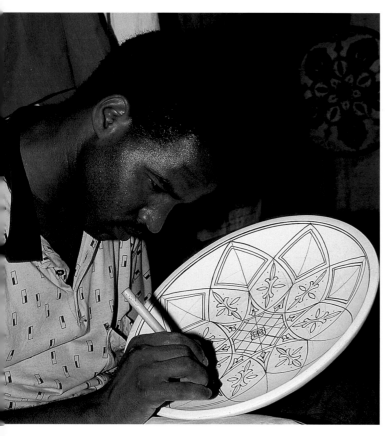

A Moroccan artist adds decorative detail to a plate. Morocco is well known for its fine pottery.

An art gallery in Kampala, Uganda, exhibits art that shows a combination of African and outside influences.

Nigeria, for example, produced some of the earliest known pottery sculptures (500 BC), and Benin in West Africa was a centre (with Nigeria) for the casting of brass and bronze. In East Africa the Masai are famous for beadwork, and in Zimbabwe the Shona people are known for their carved soapstone.

African art today has been influenced by western artistic traditions to become even more diverse. For example, western art forms, such as painting, are now widely practised in East Africa, and African patterns and colours (especially from West and North Africa) have become a major influence in European and American fashion and design. African literature has also gained worldwide appeal through the writings of authors such as Ngugi wa Thiong'o of Kenya and Chinua Achebe and Wole Soyinka, both from Nigeria. Wole Soyinka won the Nobel Prize for Literature in 1986.

● ● ● ● ● ● ➤ IN FOCUS: African rhythms

In Africa even everyday actions, such as digging in the fields or pounding grain, may be set to a rhythm and accompanied by a song. Drums too have a long history and, besides being used to create music, were once used for communication – their sound travelling over great distances. Guitars and xylophones are also a mainstay of African music, but it is people's voices that are most often heard in haunting chants or beautiful harmonies. Africa has influenced modern music too (blues music, for example, came from the working songs of West African slaves in the United States), and has produced its own international stars such as Youssou N'Dour (Senegal), Thomas Mapfumo (Zimbabwe) and Salif Keita (Mali).

A traditional healer in Nigeria uses natural materials and ingredients to treat a patient. Traditional medicine is widely used in Africa and is based on knowledge passed down over hundreds of years.

RELIGION IN AFRICA

Broadly speaking, Africa can be divided into three religious belief systems. Islam dominates the north of the continent, while Christianity is the main religion in the rest of Africa. The third belief system, traditional religion, is found throughout sub-Saharan Africa, but is not as easy to identify. Traditional religion does not follow regular patterns, such as Sunday being a day of prayer for Christians or Ramadan a holy month for Muslims. Instead traditional religion is interwoven with aspects of everyday life and centres round a spiritual belief in nature and ancestor worship. People may pray to their ancestors for a good harvest, for example, or visit a spirit diviner to bring them luck before starting up a new business venture. In African traditional religion, the followers' beliefs are passed down by the elders of the community, as they have been for hundreds of years, and ritual and sacrifice play an important part. Nowadays many Africans follow both traditional beliefs and more mainstream faiths such as Islam or Christianity. This mixing of faiths makes religion in Africa very complex.

CONQUEST AND TRADE

In North Africa, Islam is almost universal, and it is estimated that a third of all Africans are Muslims. Islam was introduced to Africa by means of conquest and trade. In North Africa, it spread rapidly from around 700 AD, as Arab peoples gained control of the region from the then

Roman Empire. Beginning in Egypt, Arabic territory spread west and soon reached as far as the Atlas mountains in Morocco. Islamic beliefs followed, and by the eleventh century most North Africans were Muslims.

A mosque in the desert town of Douz in Tunisia. Tunisia was one of the first parts of Africa to become predominantly Islamic.

Islam's spread into other parts of Africa was slower and was closely linked to trans-Saharan trade routes. Muslim traders from North Africa established small communities in sub-Saharan Africa from where they exchanged goods with local merchants and rulers. Gradually some of the local merchants and rulers converted to Islam to show solidarity with their fellow merchants and over time Islam spread into the wider community. Traders also brought Islam from across the Indian Ocean to the coast of Africa. Mombassa on the Kenyan coast, for example, has a large Muslim population.

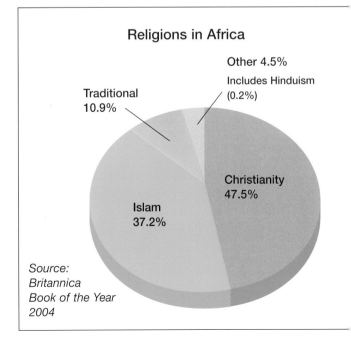

Religions in Africa

Other 4.5%
Includes Hinduism (0.2%)

Traditional 10.9%

Christianity 47.5%

Islam 37.2%

Source: Britannica Book of the Year 2004

FACT FILE

In 2004, Christianity was the main religion in many African countries, including Ethiopia, South Africa, Namibia, Kenya, Ghana and Zimbabwe. Several distinctly African branches of evangelical Christianity have gained particular popularity in recent decades.

CHRISTIAN MISSIONS

Christianity was mainly introduced to Africa by European Christian missionaries. As well as teaching Christianity and founding new churches, missionaries were frequently involved in running schools, health clinics and hospitals in colonial Africa. In addition, Egypt and Ethiopia have a long history of Christianity through their Coptic Churches. These date back as far as the fourth century AD (when Christian beliefs were introduced by the Romans).

OTHER RELIGIONS

Africa has relatively small communities of other religions, besides the main three (Christianity, Islam and Traditional). Hinduism, Sikhism, Bahai and Judaism are all present, mainly in eastern and southern Africa. Rastafarianism, a politico-religious sect of Jamaican origin, is also linked to Africa. Rastafarians believe that the former Emperor of Ethiopia (1930-1974), Haile Selassie, was a messiah and a champion of the black race. They continue to worship Haile Selassie in the belief that he will one day secure their passage back to Africa.

SPORT IN AFRICA

No matter where you are in Africa, people talk about sport with great knowledge and passion. Soccer is the most popular sport, and local teams always receive good support. In Cairo, a

A village soccer match in rural Burkina Faso. These boys have a shop-bought football, but others create their own using old plastic bags tied together in a ball with string.

local match can leave the normally crowded streets deserted. The main competition for African football is the African Nations Cup, which is held every two years. Nigeria, Cameroon, South Africa, Senegal, Morocco and Tunisia have also played in the World Cup finals, and in 2002 Senegal reached the quarter-finals. In 2010 the World Cup finals will be held on the African continent for the first time, when they are hosted by South Africa. Other sports are not nearly as big in Africa, although in southern Africa rugby and cricket are popular and South Africa is among the world's leading teams in both sports.

FACT FILE

Anthropologists have estimated that the average Kalenjin person from Kenya's highlands could outrun 90 per cent of the rest of the human race.

●●●●●●● ▶ IN FOCUS: Run for Africa

If Africa dominates the world in any sport it is in running. Several records belong to African runners. They do especially well in long-distance running (over 800 m), and completely dominate some events. For example, at 5,000 m Kenyan athletes hold 48 of the fastest 100 times, while Moroccans hold 23 and Ethiopians 18. Many of the finest runners, such as Haile Gebrselassie of Ethiopia, were born and raised at high altitude. The thinner air found at altitude contains less oxygen and is thought to help their performance, as it makes the body work much harder.

Whatever the reasons for their success, African runners continue to astonish and outpace the world with their extraordinary ability.

Haile Gebrselassie (Ethiopia) and Paul Tergat (Kenya) cross the line in the 10,000 m final at the Sydney Olympics 2000 – the closest final ever.

5. NATURAL RESOURCES IN AFRICA

AFRICA IS RICH IN NATURAL RESOURCES, BUT THEIR DISTRIBUTION is very uneven. South Africa and Nigeria, for example, have an abundance of resources, while Kenya and Tunisia are relatively resource-poor. Natural resources were central to the European colonization of the continent. For instance, the British sought control of precious minerals such as gold, diamonds and copper in southern Africa.

METALS AND MINERALS

Africa leads the world in the production of several important minerals and has a major share in the production of others. At the start of the twenty-first century, the continent accounted for around 80 per cent of the world's platinum, 54 per cent of its diamonds, 24 per cent of its gold and 22 per cent of its uranium. Africa also produces large proportions of many precious metals, such as palladium, chromite, cobalt, manganese, vanadium and titanium.

South African miners work deep underground to extract gold, one of the country's main minerals.

In West Africa, the land-locked country of Chad has large oil reserves in an area known as the Doba Basin, but there used to be no way of getting the oil to the ocean for export. Then, in July 2003, a 1,050 km (650 mile) pipeline was completed, from the Doba Basin across Chad and through neighbouring Cameroon to an offshore oil export terminal. The project is one of the most ambitious natural resource projects ever completed in Africa. As the pipeline reaches full production, it is expected to bring great economic benefits to Chad (one of Africa's poorest countries).

Oil workers drill in Chad as the country's first oil begins to flow. Thousands of new jobs will be created by Chad's oil industry.

These metals have various uses, such as in electronic circuit boards (for telephones and computers) or to make metal alloys (when two or more metals are combined). South Africa dominates the continent's mining industry and has become one of Africa's wealthiest countries as a result. Johannesburg, in particular, is a city 'built on gold', which has grown because of the gold and coal deposits situated nearby.

Several African countries have significant mineral reserves that are as yet untapped because of infrastructure problems (lack of roads or rail) or political instability. The Democratic Republic

FACT FILE

South Africa has the world's deepest mine, in Carletonville, Guateng province. The Western Deep Levels gold mine reaches a maximum depth of 3,581 m (11,749 feet).

of the Congo (Congo D.R.), for instance, has particularly large reserves of several important minerals, including limestone, palladium, copper, gold, manganese, uranium, diamonds and iron ore.

FORESTRY

Trees are an important natural resource throughout most of Africa, mainly used to provide energy in the form of wood fuel and charcoal or for construction materials. Such uses have placed enormous pressure on Africa's forests – between 1990 and 2000 Africa accounted for 56 per cent of the global reduction in forest cover. In many areas (especially around towns and cities) tree cover is so low that people must now walk several kilometres just to collect enough wood to cook their next meal.

Tropical timber is prepared for the construction industry in Burundi.

Compared with other parts of the world, commercial forestry is relatively small-scale in most of Africa. However some central and West African countries, such as Cameroon, the Democratic Republic of Congo and Ghana, earn substantial amounts from forestry. Cameroon, for example, earned about US$430 million from forestry exports in 2002, which was around 23 per cent of its total export earnings. Commercial logging in Africa is expected to increase, as new access roads open up remaining areas of forest. Historically, governments across Africa have made little effort to tackle the problem of forest loss. In recent years this has changed and most of them have realized that they must control deforestation and promote replanting in order to make forests a sustainable resource for the future.

FACT FILE

In the year 2000, 91 per cent of all the wood used in Africa was burnt as fuel.

The fishing fleet at rest in the Moroccan port of Agadir. Morocco has rich fishing waters off the West African coast.

FISHERIES

The waters off much of Africa's coastline are rich in fish and this provides a valuable natural resource for coastal communities. The marine fisheries of West Africa and southern Africa are especially productive and in 2000 produced around 2.7 million tonnes (2.65 million tons) of fish – about 3 per cent of the global marine catch. Inland fisheries on Africa's lakes and rivers are also important. For example, Lake Victoria in East Africa supports a growing fish export industry (mainly selling to Europe and the Middle East) as well as providing fish for local communities. The lake is under threat, however, from over-fishing, pollution and the introduction of foreign species (fish and plants not native to the lake). Kenya, Tanzania and Uganda, which share Lake Victoria, are cooperating to try and conserve the lake ecosystem but some damage, such as the loss of over half the native cichlid fish species, is irreversible.

VITAL ENERGY

Energy is an essential resource for economic development, but in many African countries energy supplies are seriously lacking or unreliable. Even oil-rich countries, such as Nigeria, suffer regular power shortages because they tend to export their oil to earn foreign income, rather than using it to meet their own needs. In southern Africa, coal provides an important source of energy, while in South Africa it produces around 90 per cent of the country's electricity and is even converted into a form of oil.

POWER FROM WATER

Hydro-electric power (HEP) is a major source of electricity in Africa and it provides over 95 per cent of electricity for ten countries. These include Ghana, Ethiopia, Mozambique, Democratic Republic of the Congo and Uganda. As African economies continue to develop, the demand for power grows, and there are plans for new dams to increase HEP production across the continent. In Uganda, two dams along the River Nile

The Nile crashes over Itanda Falls near its source in Uganda. The Ugandan government plans to use the power contained in the falling water to generate hydro-electric power (HEP).

will more than double electricity production when they are completed. Ethiopia, Kenya and Angola are other countries that wish to build new dams.

The Inga scheme on the Congo river is still at the planning stage. This would involve a series of HEP stations along the Congo river and would be the world's biggest HEP project. If completed, the Inga project would distribute electricity across Africa through a network of power lines that would meet the current needs of the entire continent. Critics of the project say that the local environment and the whole of the Congo river would be badly affected by the proposals. They are also concerned that the electricity generated would go to large urban centres and not benefit Africa's rural poor who have no access to electricity. In the past, large HEP projects have run into funding and management problems, so it remains to be seen whether the Inga project will be built at all.

● ● ● ▶ IN FOCUS: Tapping the Earth's energy

In Kenya, electricity is generated using geothermal energy from beneath the Earth's surface. Volcanic activity in the Rift Valley produces super-heated steam that is captured and used to drive generating turbines. Kenya is currently planning or completing several new geothermal power stations. These will increase the amount of electricity produced in this way to around 18 per cent of the country's total by 2017.

Olkaria geothermal power station in Kenya provides a renewable source of energy to meet Kenya's fast-growing demand for electricity.

6. THE AFRICAN ECONOMY

AFRICA IS THE WORLD'S POOREST REGION, WITH AROUND HALF THE continent's population living in severe poverty. Poverty is especially high in sub-Saharan Africa, where 47 per cent of the people were living on less than US$1 per day in 2001. North Africa is wealthier than sub-Saharan Africa, but all African economies are poor in comparison to other world regions. In 2002, for example, the United States' economy was around twenty times bigger than that of all African nations combined. Africa's biggest economy, South Africa, was less than 7 per cent that of the UK in 2002 and just 1 per cent that of the United States.

Wealth and poverty often exist side by side in Africa's big cities, as shown here in the Kenyan capital Nairobi.

FACT FILE

Namibia and Lesotho are two of the most unequal societies in the world, with the richest 20 per cent of the population enjoying an income around 120 times greater than that of the poorest 20 per cent.

INEQUALITIES

The wealthiest economies in Africa are those of South Africa, Botswana and Namibia, where average annual incomes are above US$7,000 and as high as US$10,000 in South Africa. However, within economies, the level of wealth varies dramatically. In Zambia, for instance, just 20 per cent of the population controls 57 per cent of the country's wealth, while the poorest 20 per cent share only 3 per cent. The wealthy in Africa enjoy more luxurious lifestyles than most people in richer countries such as the USA, Japan or the UK, because the cost of living is much lower. For Africa's poorest, however, life is dominated by hunger, illness and insecurity.

PRIMARY COMMODITIES

Many of Africa's economies rely on producing raw materials, such as minerals, or agricultural goods like tea or cotton. These are known as primary commodities and they are mainly exported from Africa to manufacturers in Europe and North America. The primary commodities are processed into more valuable products or manufactured goods, some of which are then sold back to African countries. This pattern has led to a gradual transfer of wealth from Africa to the rest of the world.

A reliance on primary commodities also creates an economy vulnerable to changes in world prices caused by the development of new materials or the discovery of alternative supplies. With agricultural commodities, factors such as the weather can play a vital role. The price of coffee, for example, can rise or fall by as much as 260 per cent in just a few months. In general, the price of primary commodities has fallen over the years, so many African economies are earning less today than they did several decades ago.

AGRICULTURE

Agriculture dominates most African economies, employing over 80 per cent of the workforce in countries such as Sudan, Rwanda, Niger and Zambia. In drier parts of the continent, pastoral farming (with livestock such as cows, goats and sheep) is the most widely practised form of agriculture. Pastoralists

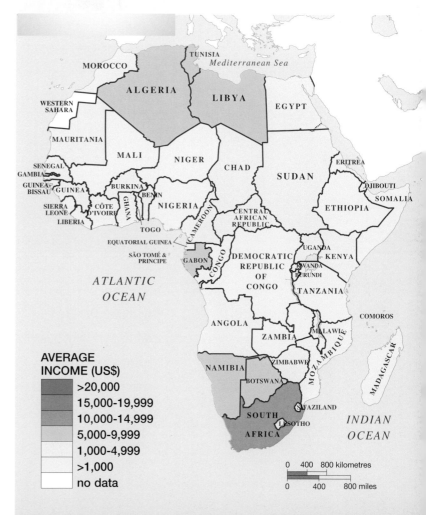

FACT FILE

Ethiopia relies on coffee for around 54 per cent of its export earnings.

Bales of cotton are weighed in Sudan before being transported to markets around the world. Cotton is one of Sudan's most important exports.

AVERAGE INCOME (US$)
- >20,000
- 15,000-19,999
- 10,000-14,999
- 5,000-9,999
- 1,000-4,999
- >1,000
- no data

Small plots, such as this one in Sierra Leone, are typical of agriculture across much of Africa. Most of the food grown will be eaten by the family or sold in local markets.

(pastoral farmers), like the Fulani or Tuareg people of West Africa, can travel great distances as they follow the rains in search of fresh pasture for their livestock. Where rainfall is more reliable, settled agriculture is more common. The majority of farmers grow a mixture of crops, some to meet their own needs (subsistence farming) and others to sell.

CASH CROPPING

During colonial rule, African farmers were encouraged to grow certain crops that were in high demand by the colonial powers. These became known as 'cash crops' because they were grown solely to be sold. The main cash crops included cotton, cocoa, tea, coffee, groundnuts, rubber and tobacco, and many African countries still rely on these today. Kenya, for example, depends on tea for much of its income, Sudan and Egypt rely heavily on cotton, and cocoa accounts for around a quarter of Ghana's export earnings. Cash crops were originally sold to the former colonial powers, but today they are sold on the world commodity markets, along with produce from other parts of the world.

Tea is a major African cash crop. This picker is in Kenya, the continent's leading tea producer.

FACT FILE

The value of flowers exported from Kenya increased from US$39 million in 1991 to US$175 million by 2002.

In recent years Kenya, along with South Africa, Egypt, Morocco and Zimbabwe, has begun producing new cash crops such as vegetables, spices, fruits and flowers (known collectively as horticulture). These command a higher price than traditional cash crops and are less vulnerable to changes in world commodity prices. Unfortunately they also require specialized farming techniques. They therefore tend to be grown by large commercial farms (many of which are foreign-owned) because local farmers are unable to afford the required equipment. However, the farms do create jobs, as labour is needed to pick, process and pack the crops. In Kenya, over 135,000 people are employed in the horticulture industry, which accounted for 35 per cent of agricultural exports in 2003.

MANUFACTURING

In most African countries, there is a relatively small manufacturing industry and many goods are imported. There are assembly plants in some countries where goods, such as motor vehicles, are put together for the local

●●●▶ IN FOCUS: Fair trade

During the 1990s, new fair trading systems were established. Fair trade works by sourcing crops such as tea, coffee, cocoa and sugar from local farmers rather than large commercial farms. The local farmers are given a guaranteed price for their goods and paid part of their income in advance. This allows them to plan for the future and means they can afford fertilizers and machinery to help improve their harvests. Fair trade products are marked with a special logo so that consumers in Europe or North America can choose whether to support local farmers in regions such as Africa.

market. However, Egypt, Kenya, Nigeria, South Africa and Morocco have quite big export manufacturing sectors. Morocco and Egypt, for example, are well known for producing clothing and textiles. The export of such goods remains mainly to former European colonial powers, with the United States and Japan also being key trading partners. The rest of Africa's manufacturing industry mainly produces goods for African markets, such as cleaning products, educational materials and household items.

SERVICES

Apart from essential services, like teaching and healthcare, Africa's service sector is relatively undeveloped. This is changing, however, as new technologies, such as mobile phones and the Internet, help to create new jobs and business opportunities. Communications, banking, and the travel and tourism industry have also taken advantage of new technologies and grown rapidly in recent years to become important employers in several African countries. South Africa has the most advanced service sector and also has the Johannesburg Securities Exchange, which in 2004 was the world's sixteenth biggest stock exchange.

Internet use in Africa has grown rapidly in recent years. Most people cannot afford their own computers so instead they visit an Internet café such as this one in Cairo, Egypt.

INFORMAL ECONOMY

One important element in any African economy is the informal sector. This covers the millions of people who provide goods and services for local communities and businesses, but without paying taxes like businesses in the formal sector. This represents a loss of tax revenue, so many governments see the informal economy as a major problem. (Because the informal economy deals mainly in cash, it is difficult for governments to monitor their business, as there are no records.) In Nairobi, the Kenyan capital, the city council has frequently tried to drive informal traders out of the city.

Informal sector workers in Malawi sell fruit to bus passengers. Millions of Africans earn their living doing such work.

A member of the Zabbaleen in Cairo, Egypt, sorts through the city's waste, looking for items that can be reused or recycled.

Other governments have been more tolerant of the informal sector and have recognized the valuable contribution it makes to the wider economy and society. For example, in Cairo, Egypt, a community of up to 60,000 informal sector waste collectors, known as 'the Zabbaleen', collect and recycle an estimated 60-80 per cent of the city's rubbish. In most African countries the informal sector performs similar important roles (such as transportation, water provision and waste management), many of which are vital to the proper functioning of the formal economy. For this reason, the informal sector will continue to be important for the foreseeable future.

7. AFRICA IN THE WORLD

AFRICA'S REPUTATION IN THE WORLD IS EXTREMELY MIXED. SOME SEE **it as a continent of great beauty, of incredible wildlife, of fascinating people, but for others Africa is plagued by poverty, disease, war and disasters. Few people associate Africa with business, trade, or major world influence. In many ways they are right. Africa accounts for less than 2 per cent of world trade, and this proportion has been declining since 1980 when it was around 5 per cent. Africa is also under-represented within global organizations.**

CULTURAL CONNECTIONS

However, despite its lack of economic power, Africa has a strong influence on other aspects of life around the world. Blues and jazz music, for example, have their roots in rhythms and songs that were originally taken to the United States by West African slaves.

A jazz band plays in Nairobi, Kenya. Jazz is an American form of music that has its roots in Africa. It is now popular across the world.

Africa has also influenced the global fashion and textile industries, with African colours, patterns and styles being frequently used by designers across the world. Tourism is another way in which Africa has become more globally integrated – since 1995 Africa's tourist industry has been growing faster than the global average. Southern Africa and East Africa

receive the bulk of Africa's tourists because of their unrivalled combination of wildlife and beaches. They also have better infrastructure (including airports, roads and hotels).

AID AND DEBT

One of Africa's main links to the wider world is international aid. Aid is normally received in the form of money borrowed from wealthier countries, international organizations (such as the European Union) or global banks. It is nearly always loaned for projects like the building of a new dam or road, or to meet specific needs such as training more teachers or improving health facilities. Many African economies need this financial aid in order to develop, but then fall behind on the loan repayments and build up large debts. Mauritania's debt, for example, is 1.3 times greater than its national income. Debts are crippling for poor economies because scarce income is used to make loan repayments, instead of being invested in the future development of the country. Each day Africa repays around US$40 million to international organizations, banks and wealthy nations.

FOCUS ON AFRICA?

As the twentieth century drew to a close, the international community agreed that Africa must become a focus of attention for the next millennium. A combination of political instability, declining trade, and

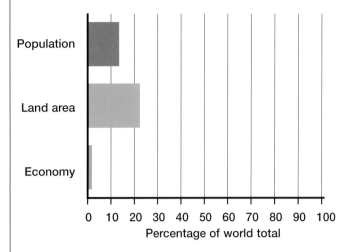

Africa compared with the rest of the world

Source: United Nations; World Bank; Britannica Book of the Year 2004

As Secretary General, Kofi Annan of Ghana has led the UN through some of the most difficult challenges it has ever faced. He continues to push for peace and development in Africa.

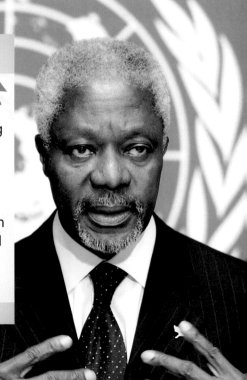

FACT FILE

In mid-2004, African countries owed almost US$300 billion. Spiralling interest rates have hugely increased their debts. For example, Nigeria originally borrowed US$5 billion; in 2004, it had already paid back US$16 billion and still owed US$32 billion.

West African regional troops from the Economic Community of West African States Cease-Fire Monitoring Group (ECOMOG) in operation in Liberia – one of many countries where ECOMOG forces have been used to restore stability.

health issues such as HIV/AIDS and malaria, had left Africa as the world's most impoverished region. Pledges were made to help overcome these problems, and to encourage reform and investment in African economies. However, there has been little sign of progress as yet.

Part of the problem has been a shift in world attention after the terrorist attacks on the United States in September 2001. Funds that might have been used to assist Africa have been diverted to deal with problems in regions where the terror threat is thought to be most serious. However, Africa has itself been the victim of terror attacks in Egypt, Kenya, Tanzania and Morocco. Although western tourists and interests are normally the main target for such attacks, many Africans have also been killed or wounded. Some experts are concerned that, if investment is not made in Africa, it could become a base for future terrorists who are angered at their issues being ignored by the wider world. Extreme terrorist organizations have been accused of recruiting and training terrorists in countries such as Sudan, Egypt and Kenya, for example.

REGIONAL STRENGTH

One way in which Africa is trying to develop is by building greater regional strength. Establishing regional trading organizations, such as the Economic Community of West African States (ECOWAS) or the Southern African Development Community (SADC), makes it easier for member countries to trade with each other because it removes, or lowers, taxes and tariffs on goods traded between these countries. Cooperation on key issues, such as transportation and energy, is also important. The East African Community (Kenya, Uganda, Tanzania) is working to improve road, rail and air links, for example. In 2002, the African Union (AU) was launched to promote economic and political cooperation at a continental level. This is considered essential to help Africa compete in a more globalized world.

● ● ● ● ● ● ● ● ➤ IN FOCUS: Instability

A major obstacle to growth and development in Africa is the instability suffered by many countries and regions. Since the 1990s, numerous states – including Rwanda, Liberia, Sierra Leone, Sudan and Somalia – have suffered wars or ongoing civil conflicts. The international community has been reluctant to become directly involved in Africa's internal conflicts but Somalia (December 1992-March 1994) was an exception. Led by the United States, an international force attempted to impose peace in Somalia, but failed to improve conditions, and withdrew when warring factions turned against them. The international community today encourages peace talks to end Africa's conflicts and provides aid to assist those forced from their homes by the threat of violence. Uganda is one country that has increased its stability by introducing political, economic and security reforms. Problems remain, but the country is now stable enough to attract international investment and to make Uganda one of the world's fastest-growing economies.

US troops entered Somalia to prevent further suffering of the Somali people, but were driven out when Somali warlords began targeting them and other foreign troops.

8. AFRICAN WILDLIFE

*F*OR CENTURIES, PEOPLE AND WILDLIFE HAVE LIVED SIDE BY SIDE in Africa. However, over the last one hundred years (and especially in more recent decades), population growth, competition for land, and the impact of human activities (including deforestation, pollution and species introductions) have placed Africa's wildlife under such pressure that in some places it may never recover.

A pygmy hunting in the Democratic Republic of the Congo. Careful management of wildlife is vital to the pygmies' way of life.

A VALUED RESOURCE?

For people such as the San of the Kalahari desert in southern Africa, or the various pygmy groups living in Central Africa, wildlife remains essential to survival. These people are hunter-gatherers who manage the environments in which they live in order to get a supply of food and most other materials they require. Because they depend so heavily on their environment, such groups value wildlife very highly and take measures to conserve and protect it. They will never hunt young or breeding animals, for instance, and they regularly move their hunting grounds to avoid exhausting any one area of its wildlife.

Africa's wildlife is not always seen as a benefit, however. In fact, many consider it to be more of a burden than a resource. Animals such as monkeys, elephants and hippopotamuses are much hated by farmers because they destroy crops and so reduce human food supplies. Predators such as lions and leopards are also loathed because they steal livestock and sometimes may even injure or kill humans. Some people even consider harmless grazers, such as zebra or wildebeest, to be a

A Masai herder keeps watch over his cattle, which share the grazing lands of Amboseli National Park in Kenya with herds of elephant.

menace because they compete with domestic livestock for pastureland. As a result of these conflicts, many animals have been exterminated or driven out of large parts of Africa in order to make way for human activities.

PROTECTED AREAS

In the 1950s and 1960s, Africa's governments realized that they must act to stop wildlife being destroyed in some parts of the continent. The main strategy was to form reserves or national parks as protected areas in which wildlife could live untroubled by human activities. Unfortunately this approach often led to increased tensions as people were denied access to lands that their ancestors had used for hundreds of years. Tensions increased further when the reserves and parks began to attract wealthy international tourists but failed to benefit local people (whose land had been lost). In Kenya's Amboseli National Reserve, the Masai even resorted to killing wildlife in protest at the government policy.

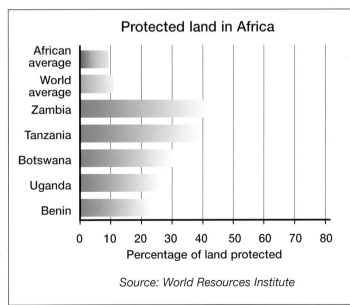

Protected land in Africa

Source: World Resources Institute

LIVING WITH WILDLIFE

Today, wildlife management in Africa is more focused on encouraging people and animals to live in harmony. Governments have realized that the best way to protect wildlife is to demonstrate its value as a resource that can benefit local people if properly protected. Tourism is one of the main ways in which wildlife can generate an income, with foreign tourists paying high prices to see birds and animals in their natural habitat.

A white rhinoceros in Nakuru National Park in Kenya. Nakuru is a sanctuary for the endangered rhino (black and white) and is surrounded by a high-voltage electric fence to keep poachers out. Across Africa, poachers reduced numbers of the more endangered black rhino from 65,000 in the 1970s to just 2,400 by the mid-1990s. By mid-2004, the numbers had recovered to 3,600 as a result of successful conservation.

However, tourism can cause considerable damage if it is not carefully managed. In Kenya's Masai Mara, for instance, the large number of tourists has forced some animals to change their behaviour patterns. Cheetahs now hunt in the middle of the day, when they are less disturbed by tourist vehicles. But the midday heat means their hunts are often less successful and this in turn threatens the survival of some cheetah families. Tourism can also be disruptive to local people, as tourist lodges compete for scarce resources such

IN FOCUS: The CAMPFIRE Project

One of the most successful approaches to living with wildlife is the Communal Areas Management Programme for Indigenous Resources (CAMPFIRE) project in Zimbabwe. This was started in the 1980s as a way for people living in the communal lands bordering national parks to benefit from wildlife. They earn income through activities such as licensed hunting, guided tours and harvesting wild produce. The income generated goes back into the local community where they decide how best to spend it. Over 250,000 people are involved in CAMPFIRE, and average incomes are estimated to have increased by around 25 per cent. Education and health facilities have improved, and people are now willing to protect wildlife because they see the animals as an asset that offers them a valuable source of income.

as fuel wood and water. In the Samburu region of Kenya, local water supplies have run dry because nearby lodges use the water to fill swimming pools and water their gardens.

An eco-tourist watches a young gorilla playing in Virunga National Park, in the Democratic Republic of the Congo. Tourist numbers are limited to reduce disruption to the gorillas and protect them from human diseases.

Eco-tourism has become increasingly popular in Africa. This form of tourism limits the number of visitors in wilderness areas and ensures that local people benefit from their stay. In the forests bordering Uganda, Rwanda and the Democratic Republic of the Congo, eco-tourists visiting the endangered mountain gorillas have helped to pay for their conservation. Gorilla numbers are increasing as a result, and had risen from 620 in 1989 to around 700 by the end of 2003.

9. THE FUTURE OF AFRICA

At the start of the twenty-first century, Africa is a troubled continent that lags behind the rest of the world in almost every way. Between 1964 and 2004, internal conflicts have cost Africa seven million lives and US$250 billion. Instability continues to be the greatest challenge to the future of the continent. In Sudan, for example, the Darfur region (an area the size of France) erupted into bloody violence in 2004 when the Sudanese government and an Arab militia group (the Janjaweed) tried to crush anti-government rebels. Millions of people were displaced and thousands were killed, injured or raped. As one of the longest modern-day conflicts, the situation in Sudan is in many ways a test case for bringing peace and security not only to its own people, but also to Africa as a whole.

Rwanda's next generation, like millions across Africa, hope for a future that will be free of violence and instability.

THE HUMAN CHALLENGE

One of the most fundamental challenges facing Africa is that of its growing population. By 2030, it will probably be home to almost 1.4 billion people (nearly double the population of 1995). Several African countries are expected to double their populations in an even shorter time, including Uganda, Rwanda and Liberia by 2015, and Chad and Mali by 2020. Such rapid population growth will place even greater pressure on Africa's already overstretched health and education facilities, especially as they continue to struggle with the impact of HIV/AIDS.

By 2002, HIV/AIDS had become the leading cause of death in sub-Saharan Africa, destroying families, weakening economies, and placing governments under extreme political pressure. Despite the obvious challenge of such circumstances, countries like Uganda have shown that – with an active public education policy – cases of HIV/AIDS can be dramatically reduced. The incidence of HIV/AIDS in Uganda fell from around 14 per cent of the population in the late 1980s to less than 5 per cent by 2003.

A poster in Sierra Leone warning people about HIV/AIDS, which has destroyed millions of lives in Africa. Encouraging greater awareness is a priority for African governments.

THE AFRICAN ECONOMY

Africa will have to generate a higher per capita income in order to meet the needs of its growing population. For many African countries, this will mean reshaping their economies and moving away from dependence on a few primary commodities. Competing for a greater share of world trade is likely to be extremely difficult, however.

South Africa has succeeded in attracting foreign investment to boost its economy. This car assembly plant in Durban makes cars for the Japanese company, Toyota.

African nations lack the power of wealthier nations and are normally unable to offer the incentives that richer governments use to attract international investment. In addition, many countries still lack infrastructure, energy supplies and skilled workers. These will all be necessary to help Africa play a greater role in the global economy and improve the livelihoods of its people in the twenty-first century.

STATISTICAL COMPENDIUM

Nation	Area (sq km)	Population (2003)	Urbanization (% population) 2003	Life expectancy at birth 2002 (in years)	GDP per capita (US$) 2002	Percentage of population under 15 years 2003	Percentage of population over 65 years 2003
Algeria	2,381,741	31,800,000	58.8	69.5	5,760	34	4
Angola	1,246,700	13,625,000	35.7	40.1	2,130	48	3
Benin	112,680	6,736,000	44.6	50.7	1,070	45	3
Botswana	581,730	1,785,000	51.6	41.4	8,170	41	2
Burkina Faso	274,400	13,002,000	17.8	45.8	1,100	47	3
Burundi	27,816	6,825,000	9.9	40.8	630	45	3
Cameroon	475,442	16,018,000	51.4	46.8	2,000	41	4
Cape Verde	4,033	463,000	55.9	70.0	5,000	41	4
Central African Republic	622,436	3,865,000	42.7	39.8	1,170	42	4
Chad	1,284,000	8,598,000	24.9	44.7	1,020	48	3
Comoros	1,862	768,000	35.0	60.6	1,690	42	3
Congo	342,000	3,724,000	53.5	48.3	980	47	3
Côte d'Ivoire	322,463	16,631,000	44.9	41.2	1,520	41	3
D.R. Congo	2,344,858	52,771,000	31.6	41.4	650	48	3
Djibouti	23,200	703,000	83.7	45.8	1,990	42	3
Egypt	997,739	71,931,000	42.1	68.6	3,810	33	4
Equatorial Guinea	28,051	494,000	48.1	49.1	30,130	44	4
Eritrea	121,144	4,141,000	19.9	52.7	890	44	3
Ethiopia	1,133,882	70,678,000	15.6	45.5	810***	45	3
Gabon	267,667	1,329,000	83.8	56.6	6,590	40	6
Gambia	10,689	1,426,000	26.1	53.9	1,690	40	3
Ghana	238,533	20,922,000	45.4	57.8	2,130	42	4
Guinea	245,857	8,480,000	34.9	48.9	2,100	44	3
Guinea Bissau	36,125	1,493,000	34.0	45.2	710	45	3
Kenya	582,646	31,987,000	39.4	45.2	1,020	42	3
Lesotho	30,355	1,802,000	17.9	36.3	2,420	42	5
Liberia	97,754	3,367,000	46.7	47.0	N/a	44	3
Libya	1,757,000	5,551,000	86.3	72.6	7,570	33	4
Madagascar	587,041	17,404,000	26.5	53.4	740	44	3
Malawi	118,484	12,105,000	16.3	37.8	580	45	3
Mali	1,248,574	13,007,000	32.3	48.5	930	47	3
Mauritania	1,030,700	2,893,000	61.8	52.3	2,220	45	3
Mauritius	2,040	1,221,000	43.3	71.9	10,810	25	6
Mayotte (France)	375	166,000	N/a	60.0	N/a	N/a	N/a
Morocco	458,730	30,566,000	57.5	68.5	3,810	33	4
Mozambique	812,379	18,863,000	35.6	38.5	1,050	42	4
Namibia	825,118	1,987,000	32.4	45.3	6,210	41	4
Niger	1,267,000	11,972,000	22.2	46.0	800	49	2
Nigeria	923,768	124,009,000	46.7	51.6	860	43	3
Réunion (France)	2,507	756,000	91.5	N/a	N/a	N/a	N/a
Rwanda	26,338	8,387,000	18.3	38.9	1,270	45	3
São Tomé & Principe	1,001	161,000	37.8	69.7	1,317	39	6

Senegal	196,712	10,095,000	49.6	52.7	1,580	44	3
Seychelles	455	81,000	49.9	72.7	18,232	29	7
Sierra Leone	71,740	4,971,000	38.8	34.3	520	44	3
Somalia	637,000	9,890,000	34.8	47.0	N/a	48	2
South Africa	1,219,090	45,026,000	56.9	48.8	10,070	32	4
Sudan	2,503,890	33,610,000	38.9	55.5	1,820	40	4
Swaziland	17,364	1,077,000	23.5	35.7	4,550	42	3
Tanzania	945,090	36,977,000	35.4	43.5	580	45	2
Togo	56,785	4,909,000	35.1	49.9	1,480	43	3
Tunisia	164,150	9,832,000	63.7	72.7	6,760	27	6
Uganda	241,038	25,827,000	12.2	45.7	1,390	49	2
Western Sahara	252,120	308,000	93.7	N/a	N/a	N/a	N/a
Zambia	752,614	10,812,000	35.7	32.7	840	44	2
Zimbabwe	390,757	12,891,000	34.9	33.9	2,400	43	3

*** Data from 2001

Sources: UN Agencies, World Bank, Social Watch and Britannica

GLOSSARY

Arid area A dry environment that receives less than 100 mm (4 inches) rainfall per year.

Caldera A volcanic crater created when the cone of a volcano collapses in on itself.

Cichlid A family of fish found in several of Africa's freshwater lakes.

Deforestation The removal of trees, shrubs and forest vegetation.

DNA A chemical that carries genetic information in a code and that is unique to each living thing.

Drainage basin The area of land drained by a river and its tributaries.

Ecosystem The contents of an environment, including all the plants and animals that live there. This could be a garden pond, a forest or the whole of planet Earth.

Eco-tourism Tourism that is sensitive to its impact on environments and local people.

HIV/AIDS Human Immunodeficiency Virus (HIV) is a deadly virus spread by unprotected sex or contaminated needles or blood supplies. It can develop into Acquired Immuno-Deficiency Syndrome (AIDS), which is fatal. Expensive drugs can keep people alive, but there is no cure.

Hominoid A member of the biological family *Hominoidea* that includes humans and apes.

Homo erectus An extinct ancestor of humans that lived around 1.5 million years ago.

Homo sapiens sapiens The scientific name of modern human beings.

Hydro-electric power (HEP) A type of energy generated by fast-flowing water moving through turbines.

Hyper-arid area An environment that receives minimal rainfall and may go several years without any rainfall at all.

Illiterate Unable to read and write.

Independence When a country wins the right to control its own affairs.

Infant mortality The number of babies, out of every 1,000 born, who die before the age of one.

Infrastructure Networks that allow communication and/or help people and the economy to function. Examples include roads, railways, electricity and phone lines.

Malaria A tropical disease transmitted to people by mosquito bites.

Mangrove A semi-submerged tropical forest found in coastal regions of the tropics.

Manufacturing sector The part of the economy that manufactures goods.

Pastoralist Person who mainly depends on livestock (e.g. cattle) for his or her livelihood.

Pygmy A member of several groups of humans who live in the forest regions of Central Africa and are shorter than average humans.

Saline A solution or water body that contains a high level of salts.

Savannah A dry-land ecosystem dominated by tropical grassland with scattered trees or bushes.

Service sector The part of the economy that provides services such as banking and retail.

Soda lake A lake that contains a high level of diluted salts such as sodium chloride.

Urbanization The process of a region or country becoming urbanized, meaning that its population increasingly lives in urban areas (towns or cities).

FURTHER INFORMATION

BOOKS TO READ:

A River Journey: The Nile Rob Bowden (Wayland, 2006)

Countries of the World: Kenya Rob Bowden (Evans Brothers, 2002)

The Changing Face of Nigeria Rob Bowden and Roy Maconachie (Wayland, 2004)

The Changing Face of South Africa Rob Bowden and Tony Binns (Wayland, 2004)

The Changing Face of Kenya Rob Bowden (Wayland, 2002)

The Changing Face of Egypt Ron Ragsdale (Wayland, 2002)

USEFUL WEBSITES:

www.survival-international.org
Survival International is a worldwide organization supporting tribal peoples.

http://news.bbc.co.uk/1/hi/world/africa/default.stm
BBC News Africa page with latest news and country profiles.

www.bbc.co.uk/worldservice/focusonafrica/
The Africa page of the BBC World Service – full of information and a link to regional magazine 'Focus On Africa'.

www.pbs.org/wnet/africa/
An educational site with interactive elements to explore the continent, its people and its wildlife.

http://allafrica.com/
An African-based information service organized by topic or region/area.
A major resource for everything African.

INDEX

ABOUT THE AUTHOR

Rob Bowden is a freelance author and photographer specializing in geographical and environmental issues and with a particular interest in less developed regions. He has been visiting Africa for over fifteen years and has written and taken photographs for several other children's books about the continent and its countries. He has also lectured in geography and development studies at Sussex, Brighton and Keele universities in the UK.